THANKSGIVING DAWN

THANKSGIVING DAWN

Poems 1970–2008

John Graber

[signature: John Graber]

BLUE BEGONIA PRESS • YAKIMA, WA

Thanksgiving Dawn
Copyright © 2008 by John Graber
Cover Stained Glass "Grace Upon Grace" by Lucy Stoyke
Cover Photo © 2008 by Midge Bolt

FIRST EDITION

ISBN: 978-0-911287-60-8
ISBN: 0-911287-60-4

Library of Congress Cataloging-in-Publication Data

Graber, John.
  Thanksgiving dawn : poems 1970-2008 / John Graber.
      p. cm.
  Includes bibliographical references and index.
  ISBN-13: 978-0-911287-60-8 (alk. paper)
  ISBN-10: 0-911287-60-4 (alk. paper)
  I. Title.

PS3607.R3226T47 2008
811'.6--dc22
2008030830

Printed in the United States of America

Blue Begonia Press
225 S 15th Avenue
Yakima, WA 98902-3821
www.bluebegoniapress.com

for Elise

What we want is not a new technique
but the old passion felt as new.

— W.B. Yeats

TABLE OF CONTENTS

I. 1970's

II. 1980's – 1990's

III. 2000's

I. 1970's

Pledge

Dark trees along the river lowlands wait;
every catch water from gully to sea they own.
They hold the high desert mountains and ridges.
Up to their knuckles in flat winter sky,
their black nervous systems click like quick
knitting needles—counting their numbers.
Like peasants they wait, bannerless now,
but like armies on orders they gather battalions.
Many are old and remember how it was
before the dark age of the bright ax bite.

Deep in their waiting, they listen to the waters
explain that water can't do it alone anymore.
Conspiring in groves, they talk of the spring
out of the earshot of huddles in houses.
Tribes of white pine and north spruce,
box elder and oak hand down to the cypress
their troubles and plans; the redwoods concur:
it will start in the south by the mesquite and olive,
first with their banners, soon to be followed by all,
spreading out of their hollows and off of their ridges.

All is in mortgage, double . . . come due.
First to the water and then to the trees.

Walking Home

Turning down from the bottoms of blue-black
gun-metal clouds, grackles fall faster
but surer than leaves or blown paper.

The day sags under what the birds bring.
Old joints, knots of my life, grow stiff and argue
to go away like these storm-warning birds.

All those still flying are wounded and tangled
in the constant slow curves of strings of rain.
The struggle is heavily up to low branches of trees.

I walk, leaning through the wind, dragging the strings,
like a wet grouse, clumsy towards a dry home.

Pegasus

A hawk was dead along the road this morning.
Bright red pushed through the dusky graveled feathers
like the bloody lump of three kittens after throwing
a burlap sack years ago. He said then, "It wasn't me."

Every day he drives the same thirteen miles
from his room to work, point to point, sitting,
telling himself, "I'll quit this soon." He never saw
a hawk so wrong and still, "like roots in air."

The road seems narrower every morning to him.
The barbed wire comes closer, and the rooms
at the ends get smaller, and he gets smaller,
and he's never stayed too long in one place.

There is a dark, wandering gorge like the track
of a root sloping off north and down to a stream
from his place, but he's never walked it.
His open suitcases won't let him.

The road is straight and gray, and the fences move in
to what he uses. His eyes push back, finding two cows
at home, corralled before the slaughterhouse.
Their steaming breath shrouds them with cold.

The cows don't help and threaten close to him
with the hard definition of naming him a brother.
"I'm not," he says, "not the hawk, either," though his jail
seems real as the hawk's, who calls him to join

and ditch across the coming traffic's lane. He would
except for the horses seen close to the edge of town—

one gray, two roan, one young—inside wire,
content to graze ..."could clear wire anytime."

He holds the road this morning and thinks
of the gorge like a root going down by his house
in a country where he's never known the land.
He holds the road. He says to himself, "This weekend."

Volkschule, 1955

to my brother, Paul

Remember how Sicilian all the postwar children were?
A Mafia in lederhosen, how their poking fingers bit.
Remember how they hated us for wearing jeans?
And being shocked at their lard sandwiches and rosaries
read for the bomb-caved convent in their town.
Remember how we hated them for hating us?
And how we talked ourselves to sleep at night
with dreams of powerful cars and language that we knew.
Remember the sewage creek behind our house?
And the rag-tag clapboard fears we engineered
across that river Styx that kept us in
and how strange we felt and how much we looked
at the long grass curves that hung over the banks
into that oily, black water that made them die.
Remember the small dogs that scared us home?
And the kicks of the gang that put us in the ditch.
Remember how we went back out of the ditch
by crossing our bridge into the field of yellow daisies
with wooden fence-slat swords and how all afternoon
the heads of thin Austrian children fell like flowers?

Kansas Steel and Stone Blues from the City

Fields have tilted vertical
and gone to gray stone walls
hung with brittle panes of steel fenced glass,
mirroring an eighth-inch depth of harvest sun.

I am, or was, a plains man,
now pale in a world of thin women.
Wind doesn't visit often here anymore,
and coming, finds nothing to move so goes on—
nothing to move but a flag in my chest
tugging southwest to an earlier place
of smell of sun's skin and rain-poxed dust.

Somewhere is there still
warm, leaning wheat nodding over
long hills and the brown knees of girls
angling sure through those gold sea swells?
Are there quick glints of minnow and slow cat
in shadows of trees by rivers in hollows
and welcomed boys bringing fish
curving out wet from their hands
and gathered to girls?

"Not My Father"

You remembered how you saw yours
through his stories ride to battle
for the soul of South Dakota,
tall and fearfully black,
omniscient, Christian knight:
"Herr Pastor."

You hear him for the first time now
stutter his thick-tongued English on the phone.
It took you thirty years and two degrees
to hear your immigrant father
asking you home to the rural parish house.
It pains you more than can be said to see him
at the other end of the line:
bald, eighth-grade seminarian,
circuit-riding immigrant preacher,
inarticulate sad old man asking you home.

The church is gray with July dust.
The house is darker than you remember
and smells of lingering invalids.
"Grüss gott, mein Sohn, mein Magister."
He takes your hand in both of his
and leads you in, after eight years, back.
You drink thin tea he offers in charity cups.
He squirms beneath your perfect grammar.
You are the tall American he shows,
after supper, to the study
to read to you and point to fewer titles
from the shelves than you remember:
"Just a small case of holy books."
You cannot speak. His face strains
for you to know that he knows, too.
Your clothes fit too tightly.
His silent insistence embarrasses.

You can't admit you hate him for his size.
He says he has read Freud—it is 1941—
you smile in approval and note to yourself,
"He couldn't have understood."
You leave the next day. "This is not my father."

Your second son is born the year your father dies.
You remember when he showed his books.
You begin your work to become "Herr Doktor."
As your sons grow older, your face grows tight.
It is hard for you to speak. You remember
how small the church was, how dark, his broken speech.

Your first son grows to be six-four.
You cannot teach him how to play.
The first time you tried sport you fell.
He never falls. Women cheer his strength.
You don't know how to act
but stutter out archaic, "That's my boy!"

Your second son hears you never say the same of him.
You are tall and strong to him. He looks like you:
dark and worried as he sees your books,
"Herr Doktor" books, across two walls.
He works hard and grows to be five-ten,
a bookish sort and brighter, younger than you were.
Your face tightens. You cannot speak.
When he is twenty, he begins to smile
and begins to hate his "not my father."

Grandfather, for my father I am sorry.
I have a small case of holy books.
Father, I am sorry.
I know my chin can never be as rough as yours
until my son . . .

St. Mary's Psychiatric

He finds a new world.
His eyes ache as walls breathe towards him
like chests of the dying.

His head reaches out from his blanket
like a hand from a cuff,
plucking and searching continents over him.

He calls out in a language of twitches
and the hesitant gestures of worn-out smiles
to armies of demons, all with his face.

He clinches hard hours of sunlight in his fists
and beats the face of those hours onto the walls
until he cripples the day with a pain that frees.

He tries to sleep like a gull fighting down
through thousands of feet of storm
to a final land of calm under bushes.

He cries out for the pure body of Jesus,
but only late when the strength of his body
wears out with his fear will he sleep.

Then his face will become a child's hand in the night,
the face of his Jesus, until fear comes again
with tomorrow's unsought reprieve of a day.

Reporting the Traumatization of Flesh
after seeing Don Luce's Vietnam photos, 1971

The face of man melts like a candle when it burns,
obeying the laws of this other erosion
that's faster with men because man is not
so patient with men as with wax.
But the end result is the same:
a change in the form. The face folds in—
child pink at first, it dries taut brown.

In one particular case
the bulk of the napalm
struck by the nose and clung
and carved in the cheek the whorl
of an ear that listens and looks
like a free-formed orchid blushing
or a maelstrom going down.

The lower half of the face
melted over the mouth.
The man passed out
and forgot to open his mouth
before the flesh congealed,
locking the words perpetually in
and up to the eyes.

The eyes too were redesigned.
Both lids shrunk when the flesh cooled
the eyes always open
and loud with speech.
The man will go blind
because eyes dry out when open so long
and unable to close their men.

The nostrils filled
with molten flesh,
holding to the hollows

like soil that clings
in island depressions
where constant winds
argue towards death.
Were it not for the *luck*
of the hole burned in
by the side of the nose
through the cheek,
providing a way
for air to the lungs,
the man would have died.

And elsewhere,
away from the particular case,
there are men who stand before mirrors
carefully combing their hair
for the image they make
as half a continent breaks up in a storm,

in a maelstrom going down,
sunk in the orchid whorl of an ear that breathes
through the cheek by the nose of one man's scar
whose face is bigger
than whole states that sink there.

Northwest of Oslo

This is not the souring bottle of Europe.

The rain comes down lightly while walking;
the road begins to push back under our feet.
There is a breathing in the ground, a clearing;
the black earth starts through snow-covered fields.

The path is white crushed rock going up
to their long house and hewn red barn,
breathing stories of harvest three hundred years long.
Hanna takes us in.
We remember looms and butchering beef;
their eyes house barns their hands know.
Their life is the rain's slow opening up;
at night we open, asleep in their rugs.
The land comes back through snow under rain.
This is a slow working up mountains,
a carving given by men before marriage.

Bjorn went up the mountains when they came;
he went as easy as rain gathers to rain.
For three years he told stories of harvest
while his fields burned out the stomachs of Germans.

Stable Fire in Time of War

Static news of rainy weather
reached me safe behind Venetian blinds
and lace curtains bought in Spain.
On the orange linen tablecloth
delicate purple flowers and dried ditch weeds
rest in a wedding present.
My bone china cup of morning coffee, half-raised,
smashed down as I shuddered.

The coffee will dry a brown rust
on my wife's sack tablecloth.
My hands will wash white again.
The shock of burning will remain.
The cup handle came off in my hand.
I will keep it to remember
what news of thirty horses burning
did to my morning.

I half-raised Venetian blinds.
Thirty screaming horses brought it home.
Three years ago I almost mailed
a hand to a president.

The Blizzard

When the storm hit,
my wife was in the kitchen playing pans.
I was in the study playing dead.

Our one room with a heater closed its door
as each of us to each became a dark ghost
conducting the blizzard between us.

Turning, we began talking to ourselves,
but sound froze as the words came out,
cutting our lips and shattering to the floor.

My wife stooped to pick all her pieces up
and place them back north in her mind
under the longest night of the year.

I put all mine like sandbags
on the tip of my tongue,
planning against a too quick thaw.

But there was no flood.
She cried slowly for days.
When she was done and green again,
my ghost had gone. I walked to the window.
Outside, the world throbbed Amazon.

I spoke all my cold words into my hands,
unpacking my mouth. They were raven words.
I wished them well as I threw their frozen wings out
to find some land where it never thaws to live.

The Gift

Two teal angle up over Bass Lake Road.

A slow blue flying heron follows,
bobbing its head on the wing beat,
yearning northeast to water.

Too big, skinny-legged, and awkward on the ground,
this bird's not built for the grace of flight
but up or coming down, is a windfall of contradiction.

My love and I and our four arms, four legs.

Tributes

Two days ago my wife said, "Come and look!"
During the night the Fishers' one cow calved.
No one knew the calf would come so soon,
but there it stood: anointed wet and black,
with all the grace of a saw-horse
jerked into life to trip our nonchalance.
It was simply morning and new joy for us
to watch him mime his mother's stoop
to eating grass, puzzling with his nose
only to give up and bang his head against her
swollen udder for food as if she'd go away
and let him die if he didn't show he wanted
milk enough "right now!" for generations more.

It perhaps was more to us because my wife
was just past due with our own first child
stretching out her young, smooth skin.
In any case, all day long we found ourselves
suddenly laughing all alone like children do,
without a cause that others know.

But yesterday, while going down to Stutzman's gorge
with a winter's load of trash, my waiting turned.
The way was through the cattle yard.
It was calving time there, too. I counted eight
hobbling, curious, Angus young and one cow down.
Surprised, I stopped, then recognized a stiff leg up.
Her neck seemed girlish, slim—as if escaping from her
body's almost comic, blown tight, almost arrogant sides
as if she ate a feast alone before the starved
and then passed out. Her head hung, eyes open,
in the barbed wire, draining from the mouth,
but altogether calm as if she made it really
through the fence. I barked the other cattle off.
Then saw birth brought her there. Some part

or parts had caught and pushed a bloody mass
of her stomach out the other hole. The dry top
of a calf's skull showed between her legs.
Her udder hung slack and loose . . . the ends
of two teats showed red. The surrounding calves
had sucked her raw as she lay dead or dying.

I drove on to the dump yard edge where as I
threw the trash bags out I shouted, cursed—prayed
my baby down—and my wife, wife again.

First Becoming Still

The feel of you in sliding summer dresses,
somewhere between winter and summer,
was coming out of a cave into sunlight
in my hand; we rolled new hills.
You looked the same as you do now.

That one particular day of the first year
when I touched you under thin dresses,
your eyes disrobed while you were still in them,
and I, a young Adam, originally knew you.
You looked the same as you do now.

I loved you then and no tyrannies ruled me;
my government wore your bold printed cotton—
beneath it the billowing breath of new children.
We arrived as close as branch to new leaf.
You looked the same as you do now.

Smooth young branch becomes with new green
clasp of soft leaf, feathering outward.
We still meet the same way we used to—
no obvious joint, limb-leaf while I see you.
You looked the same as you do now.

The Dance of the Robins

Lacing the air with their filigree of song,
baroque or rococo—it doesn't matter—
the birds own the morning
and publish what they choose.
This time, it's the ancient song and dance
for life that brings them down to earth
in a springly mating persuasion, like ours,
ignoring the wings to involve the legs
as if proving the weight Sir Robin can carry
and leap from gravity's ground were credentials
for levity's coupling. Oh, how they dance
and lock and weave the pattern of their history
here on this greening turf of eventual demise,
flirting in the dangerous cat's grass,
sticking their necks out to touch
more children into laughter.

1700 Miles to Elise

I did not always lean so forward to the page
to speak a word so far to find you
past my crowded eyes now emptied of your face
caught double in the iris and my heart.

I did not always have to find a key
unlocking my house door with you not there
to welcome in with at least a touch
of image in my eye more live than walls.

I did not always have to bear such silence
since before we met and merged and married
to unfold four more voices to embrace
within the ears' deaf-mute empty rooms.

I did not always only feel the head's weight
bearing down and table wood beneath my arms
and only non-committal clothes against my skin
and never anything but air against my face.

I did not always miss the climbing up
of children on my life with you alone,
yet now all hands would find a greeting there
for grip upon my hair, my hands, my heart.

I did not always have to arm myself
against a dearness that now threatens to dissolve
my form and words, so far away from being flesh.
I did not always hang or live on every word.

Like Land Used Up

Like a plain still holding meadow curves but brown
and seen from one personal place in the broad palm of it,
I am, with all blades stooped in a uniform lean,
like stalks crushed or blight bent wheat.
The heart went out of it, all at once, all over.
And, still, the still picture of it is waiting.
Waiting like a long dead tree waits,
sign to a whole life spent learning to stand
in one place so deep it is hard to forget.

> Once an apple orchard died without a sign
> in middle season two years and two bounty harvests
> after one sharp freeze froze earth past the deepest roots,
> killing all from the bottom up, but not before
> two years' grace wore threat out in doubled seed
> in earth that was always ready to wed.

No, not like land used up is my present plain.
It's more like dues for shallow root putting
in a too irrigated easy life—and as I say it, yes,
I am not in one place. Yes, out there past target zero
there is a green that is mine, I can tell,
like newborn fingers starting to move before the eyes—
such, such a blue child I must have seemed—
but watched, watched, the fingers begin to move
all over beyond the palms, like secrets beginning to tell.

The Inverted Physics of the Heart

In the realm of the heart,
when something is taken away,
the heart is heavy—
this is the gravity of the heart.
When something is embraced,
the heart is light—
this is the levity of the heart.
When something is gripped tightly
it leaves, and when set free
it remains.

In the realm of the heart,
resistance creates cold;
silence speaks with the greatest volume;
and time's pendulums swing unequally—
one second can be a year
and years a moment.

In the realm of the heart,
the perfectly smooth cannot be moved;
as friction increases, things slide away;
and pushing from opposite directions
splits the heart.

In the realm of the heart,
the hardest work is determined
by the least distance traveled
and how little is held or raised;
efficiency is achieved by expending
the greatest magnitude of energy
in the appreciation of small matters;
and action does not have an equal
and opposite reaction—

when two hearts meet,
they go on together indefinitely.

In the realm of the heart—
with its lever, the mind—
the heart needs no place to stand
to move the world.

The Problem

Your mother was the last room
you lived in that had a door.

She told you to go to your room,
and you did, still resenting it.

Now you are in that room, which got bigger
as you got bigger, still without any doors.

But there are windows, all high on one wall.
You see beautiful things, all over your head.

Some things fly. There seem to be no strings attached.
You cannot see what holds them up.

Even your own room's support remains a mystery.
At night you dream of one box only in space.

Then one day tears begin filling your room.
You are not really afraid until the third day.

Then, the expected reversal does not happen.
Now you are afraid. You don't know how to swim.

The water rises to right up under your chin.
You are going to die. Your life rolls before you
like film running backward. Now it is over.

In the darkness of your room you feel rumor:
all this might have happened before.

You close your eyes hard and see a bright brass ring
at your feet like a cellar door handle.

The rumor says to get down on your knees
and reach for the carrousel ring.

Making Change
after falling 25 feet

I won't tell anything new.
What I will tell
is that when your ladder slips,
flesh falls like a potato
and the accompanying mind
can do nothing to stop it.

The heart, huddling in your mouth,
will prove itself *mere*
and amazed there is no reverse.
Your spirit won't even be able
to manage the faintest trajectory.
Upside down and in the air,
clear as the mind makes change,
you'll say, "I've spent my life."

And so it is.

When your body hits,
body will become a paper cup
crushed with the water in it,
and pain will be the water,
98%,
spilling out of your voice box
in dry waves that will fill
all space with black light
until its tide recoils
like a snake hit on the road
into a stab of sleep coiling down
the drain of the world.

That black spot
in your rear view mirror
will be nothing new.

Your shocked flesh

will climb up inside your skull
and willingly close its eyes:
"O.K."

There is nothing poetic about falling.

Except, somehow, on that day,
you may be lucky,
and before the temple caves all in
your spirit may be able to get out
and wait until after the ruining,
to go on back and blink
your eyes open again
to see, face down,
singular grains of dirt
shine diamond again

as they did for me,

unstopping my ears
to receive into their confusion
my wife's clear voice again,

"John?"

held within their reaching hands,
cupped in time to catch the drowning
raven of her voice and send back
a dove from a green land flying,

"Elise?"

through the air with a strange laugh,
throaty and as deep as the mystery
of toes that still can move
and as long as the deeper mystery still
of pain running happily downhill
from where it spills, "Elise?'

"Elise!"

While in St. Peter's, Rome

I think the world
is like the feet of the Pieta
and shines out of the dark arches only
when touched by hands that believe in it.
I think that when the feet
are worn away by touch,
people will climb up the body of Christ
until he's worn onto a world of hands,
a shining marble dust,
and then the night's white, worn pearl,
river stone moon Mary will smile,
and we'll all be home.

"Say It Again, Daddy!"
Sam's Song

Inside

a grain of sand
an egg
inside the egg
a sea

inside the sea
a whale
inside the whale
a song

inside the song
a bird
inside the bird
a story

inside the story
a tear
inside the tear
a child

inside the child
a laugh
inside the laugh
all of us

inside all of us
a grain of sand.

II. 1980's – 1990's

Barbed Wire
recalling Ecclesiastes 12

If you do not understand why we sing,

before your silver cord is snapped
or golden lamp is broken
or pitcher shatters at the spring
or pulley cracks at the well,

I am sorry that your life will be
so empty of loss, so weakened by years
of not holding onto horizons,
that a breeze can't make
your spine respond as even any
wire fence in Kansas
speaks with the spirit's
constant wind parting around it
in honor of the dues it pays
for standing still and being

moved to sing the taut song
of the lovely blue ceiling of its prison,
the warm green walls and floor,
and the barb waiting just under your skin.

Holding Back

Like a bud, not of a flower, but a leaf,
this hand, not of a body, but a mind
is clenched around a tough, vague hope.

There is dried blood in the red of its grip
clasped closed around the promising green.
Something is holding back a flood of force.

There must have been a winter, winter night,
a night in winter colder than its weather.
Something, somewhere, somehow was hurt.

There was a night of this and that cause,
the kind of rain that's blown from the north
of your life and strikes your face and freezes there
across eyelids of self-pity.

Can't a man be sorry for something
besides how others have treated him? Can't he
take them out of his throat? Must he leave them
alive in the tight fists of his nervous fingers?
If so, can't he hit the goddamn wall?
Must he let them walk away from the banquet
of his pain leaving only him to pay the price?
Isn't there some degree of hope in knowledge?
Must he, stupid, follow them again into that kind
of cold hell where he kisses the frozen metal
of his memory, leaving skin?

Believe in the Eyes

I cannot say the last time I relaxed with you,
the last time your sun woke on all my pale skin,
the last time my jaw went down and lips out,
hands rolled over on their backs and opened
for any idea or thing you might place in them.
I cannot say the last time that my pride
quit making impossible demands on your response.

I have been so little for so long, I am like
a stubborn starving child that wants one food
and will not open his mouth until it arrives,
proving how loved and known and powerful he is:
a prideful little shit of forty years. And yet,

I can look in the mirror of these words and see,
in spite of all the sad poems and "unloved" nights,
see that around my eyes, the poem of my face,
the eyes of my poems, there has been humor
enough to get hurt into writing line after line
of sadness on the paper into line after line
of laughter around the eyes. Don't listen to me.

Believe in the eyes.

Solidarity
February 9, 6:45 P.M.

Air stiffens in the nose.
It's been snowing so much
that every second day the dogs
must revisit around each tree.
Even the healthy walnuts look like sick elms—
with all their lower branches hanging down.

The whole world's gone inside,
dreaming of the heart opening up and loosing
its geese to dare Canada again with a faith
that the flush on the face of this February sunset
is not put-on, but real
as the undiscriminated larval ghosts at the bottom
of the frozen Saskatchewan mating pools are real

and ache to rise up from the depths through strata
of ever warmer layers of water and become nymphs
aching to rise up to the occasion of air
through the gauzy-lit band and break through the silver-
backed mirror of the surface as Mayflies
aching to rise into their one day
of long sun and ache as I ache
to fly May again.

Sounding February

This is the first day the road has steamed
since mid-September. At eight o'clock
the angle of the sun has turned the snow to skipping
sparks across its waves to greet the eye.

Stubborn, stiffened leaves of oak still hang
but soften their final few degrees toward fluid brown.

The air has warmed enough to call wind, "breeze."

My North Shore indoor potted spruce
puts forth its first phosphorescent needle tip
of tentative green and makes me six years old.

Forty years of winter fall from me like water
streaming from a leaping dolphin's curve.

Reach

Reaching just below the ground to where
the weed can be pulled without breaking.
Reaching to where by bending it over and pinching,
just so, the wild mushroom stem will break
clean without lifting out part of the root.
Reaching just high enough on the asparagus stalk
to snap it with a turn and lift of the wrist.

Reaching into your wife's home of words and failing.
But then going on reaching to find her face
foremost and hold it between your hands and gently
shake all the snow down from her limbs, shake
all the red and yellow leaves, shake all the ripe fruit,
shake free the spring of her hands' silence singing,
reach back into the home of words.

August Garden

Enough feminine licorice air
exults from a single row of basil
to canopy half the garden.

Alongside, even the heavy-handed dill
is overcome and has to rely on its flashy
star-burst flower to catch the eye
and send the tongue searching its memory
for the exact place on the lower lip where
astringency was left after teeth split the seed.

The surrounding disheveled bed of tomato vines
looks like the refuse of a broken fast
except for its galaxy of exhausted suns
remaining rich on the storm-pressed ground.

This is a good place for well-worked
love to walk, carefully placing his feet.

Like Growing Potatoes
"present at the creation"

First you dig a trench nine inches wide
by six deep and rake in some fertilizer.
Next reach into the bag beside you and select
a planet—Mercury, Venus, Earth, whatever.
If it's the size of an egg or so, put it in.
If it's bigger, like Jupiter, cut it so no more than
three eyes are showing and placed to look up.
Then, cover everything over halfway, just three inches.
Wait a week or two until the eyes peek through.
Then cover them over the rest of the way.
Now, every few days walk down to the trench and see
if the eyes have become leaves reaching for light.
When you see them, it's time to weed and be patient
a couple months more until the plants' purple blooms
suddenly fade and seem to wither down
the rest of every plant into what looks like
rotting piles of hopeless disease.
Here faith steps in. Though half unbelieving,
walk with your shovel to the stump of any stem
and back off nearly a foot. With your boot, press down
on the shoulder of the shovel. Push deep,
even with the ground, and tilt back . . . Wait!
If at all possible, go find a kid to watch.

Now, pull the handle back, slowly lift and turn,
spill out on the ground
                       The Bear
                          The River
                              Orion!

Watching through Three Windows before Leaving

"May God us keep From Single vision and Newton's sleep."
— William Blake

Again, this morning, through this window,
everything is perfectly there:
there in the glare of silver
sun behind a frost of cloud
and there, drooping from each branch,
the systematic walnut leaves—
shadowing leaves shivering
beside the darker, steady, deeper green
shadowing leaves splayed
from akimbo limbs
of the erratic white ash.

And clearly, closer in, through this window,
these turned white pillars of our porch
and their bric-a-brac of trim
are figures of bride and groom and wedding—
ours—before our entry into marriage to this
high brick house: hundred-year-old monument
to nothing dead or dying, but too soon left monument
to the continuing play of musical chairs with families
and houses all over the world of Time, unblinking,
and even so, this morning,
through the big windows we are watching . . .

watching everything be perfectly there:
there, as the garland blessing of early lilacs
and, there, as the wild grape leaves clamber
over the bushes after the blooms have gone
and, there, the grapes themselves, lovely clusters
of tarnished beads before the shining tongue's shining
of the tart burst, and always, here and now,
the birds, filling the trees, like this morning's
pair of mourning doves calling together today
into a song, which sings, "fade, fading . . .
fading, fade," and clearly cleans the eye.

Thanksgiving Dawn

For more than a month now the flies have slept,
but this morning the first all-night stove has warmed
the house enough to wake their buzz for dawn.

Already a hawk is up and soaring its canny,
seeming nonchalance, waiting for any lively move
in the fields caught in the quadrants of his eyes.

Down to earth but further out, the lake
of flat cast pewter is, along the nearer shore,
hammered silver by an incoming breeze,

while the light across the land is such
that each opaque object is caught in a crystal
moment somewhere between Kansas and Oz.

And, even as I say it, the last traces
of night's tenacious monochrome are overcome
by revolutions among the surviving greens.

Here, now, just off the porch, the surrounding
curtain of lilacs that hold their leaves so long
has finally dropped enough of its local color
to clearly show the story of a dozen nests—
the songs we lived in all last summer.

Speaking of the Time

In the dark
when I touch your face
in the dark
with my palm
when I touch your hip
with my palm
in the dark
a layer of dark
is taken away.

And when my hand
slides over the world of you, then
layers of what is not you
come away with the draw of my hand
just as your hand visits away
layers of what is not me.

I am not speaking of bodies or clothes.

I am speaking of time.

How very important it is
to take off all the layers of time,
all the not me, not you,
to take off with the touch of a hand
all the layers of darkness, all the veils
of love's forgotten appointments.

In My Hands

The town across the lake
and all its lights
are in my hands.

The splash of stars
and the hidden moon
revolve here in my hands.

The wind's
legions of leaves
and all their spring trees
sway together in my hands.

The sight of you standing—
the children in your eyes,

the thought of your turning,
the breath of your touching

is all so much bigger
than anything
in my hands.

Drinking America

I've drunk America like a glass of water
when I expected wine.
Taken the battered, enamel cup of Iowa,
hung from a working windmill,
and drunk an oat harvest, taking turns,
drinking America like a glacier in the eye.
Thoughtlessly drunk it with a handful
of pain pills—sip, swallow, back to work.
I've drunk America like a grapevine in June
and felt it all the way up from deep roots
go out through the arms to clusters
of fingers . . . thank you, thank you!
Sometimes even while making love
with my free wife, forgetting
even as I drank, I've drunk it.
Drunk it poor and drunk it rich.
Drunk it in New York, Chicago,
and drunk it in over forty states
from cabin springs, Kansas days,
Florida swamps, Cascade streams,
and now by the Mississippi I take it in.
And all along the way, before the memory
of the crowning heads of our three children
being born, I've paused with the skull of it
at my lips and then, OH! drunk it,
toasting America to them as I drank
it for years like a vote, a paycheck
forgotten to wait for, a spade-fork full
of the surprise of new potatoes,
a careless speech, a flag.

Subrosa

along the Mississippi at Lake Pepin

A wood duck flies from cover for water,
a brush stroke of cloud cruises south,
children's stripped play-clothes lie on the lawn,
a red-leafed tree that's been there all night
blocks the view of the lake and the barge
brunting the deep channel's water before it,
lifting the food from the floor of the river,
waking with miniscule odors the fish
sleeping as fish do in their pockets of safety.

These are the isinglass layers of May morning,
peeled back by the day's awakening through the eyes,
revealing a man in the cold air of dawn, then,
hiding him again under a day of his moving
from place to place as if he knew what he did—
lifting the food from the floor of the river.

Leaning Forward

Leaning forward into a question mark
of sunshine through a February window
and backed by the shadow he makes behind him
on shelves of this and that that he has done,
he has forgotten the question.

Once it seemed easier to get up into morning,
wash and dress, and wait for the bones to heal.
Once he wasn't waiting for the corners of walls
to come together or doors to appear, waiting
for windows that weren't mirrors, or waiting
for moments that were beds he could get out of.
Once he wasn't waiting to speak and recognize
his own voice say, "This is so!" and believe it.
Once he could see the world instead of think it.
But now everything seems curled back on itself
like a mind run over that's unable to reach
or a hand that forgets the way out of a pocket
or a foot that sees anywhere to step is wrong.

And the quandaries still go round and round,
until his signature twists into a question mark.

A Dictionary of Anhedonia

Quite simply:
Sleep is the meaning of life.
Resisting gravity becomes a bad idea.
Creative thought concludes a bathrobe is a wardrobe.
Sudden insight notes that no one needs to shave.
Existential choice puzzles between coffee now or later.
Discovery sighs that baby powder *does* cool the flaming creases.
Making love is staying on your own side of the bed.
Simultaneous orgasm yawns and stretches at the same time.
Social conscience smells your armpits.
Civic responsibility keeps your arms down.
Working out is a productive round-trip to the bathroom.
Anticipation waits for your dog to check if you're breathing.
Breakthrough gets up by eleven.
Relapse goes to bed before eight.
Optimism believes you'll think of something you can do.
Pessimism remembers that you don't do it well.
Fear guesses you might be made of glass.
Hope insists you will respect yourself again.
Faith knows faith is still out there somewhere offering itself to you.
Love bets the love surrounding you is just enough to contain your
       reasons to die.

Death Doesn't Advertise

Wake in peace enough to keep your eyes closed.
Look through your eyelids and see on the inside
the color of every human being.

Wake into the morning and feel all the points,
edges, and curves of your body touching the bed,
where it's safe to stay, slow and weighty,
as the day opens up with sounds of water
tapping in the sink or roiling from distant trains
or hissing down white noise from a passenger jet,

while maybe your love is making coffee love to you
after all those stumbling years of throwing pain
back and forth inside what's now a stronger love
that seems it's always been warm folded clothes,
raked leaves, stains of new mown grass on shoes,

and stars on stars strewn across domestic skies
full of the scent of foods you can take up in your hands:
constellations of curry, oregano, rosemary, garlic,
cream, and each other. Take it all up in your hands—

such a rich waking in peace enough to keep still and see
through your eyelids the color of every human being.

Except for this morning, before leaving your bed,
feel your eyelids become a heavy screen as mine did
when from left to right I reread the images
projected from last night's TV news:
a long line of dark men, women and children,
all seated in front of a chalk white wall . . .

such bright spring clothing. See that they have no hands.
Remember the various lengths of machete-hacked arms
that each person, so dark, raises up to you

before that wall, so white. See black Easter
candles without flame, there in Sierra Leone,
just inside your eyes.

On Seeing William Blake
on the Cover of *National Geographic*

The boy's tarnished eyes
stare at a remote dream of heaven
in the pit of the photographer's stomach.

His cane-sized black arms
cradle a two-week-old white lamb
whose bone-thin legs hang down
like slow pendulums.

This white lamb held by this black boy.
These dark eyes and blood shot whites.
These long legs never grown into.
This broad forehead of William Blake

raised once more to look at the angels
silently hovering above the eyes
of a nameless boy on a magazine cover.
This lamb. This exhausted tiger.

What Wonder If This Birdsong

What wonder if this birdsong
flowing like white water
over this morning
awakened all the stones.

What wonder if these songs
freed thanks that moved
the thousand hearts locked
in these tiny mountains.

What wonder if these stones
were only waiting for a people
to find songs inside to sing
in harmony with their praise.

What wonder if the next stone
you see sees you and stares
until you pick it up but
refuses to sing for you.

What wonder if it will
not jump out of your hand
unless your tongue tastes on it
the grayness of your life.

What wonder if it waits for you
to smell on its other side
a sudden evening of death.
What wonder if it leaps

then from your hand and strikes
the grass with a muffled thump
that sounds just like the last
or first beat of your life.

Thanks to the Sky

Just once, up in the morning, I looked up
to angels and saw my perfected family there,
myself included, all of us bending over
at the stiff-backed angle one assumes for viewing
over the edge of life into a coffin.
That's a lot of eyes to live with.

And there, the one who seems the least afraid
of my future is a grandfather I never saw on earth.
He's so short his back has to be straighter,
his huge hands are right on the rim of the sky,
and his head like a strange sun and moon
layer over each other rising at the same time,
coming up like an exclamation point
for the sentence of life they are all breathing down
with their eyes like prayers for breeze blowing through
the still green wheat of me again.
They like dead mornings even less than I.

They look through all the desiccated
surface of the world of me, all the shriveled skins
of the strange-shaped country I live in,
wrapped up in my body, while for years
they have been building a cathedral in my chest,
a first, best bed deep in my belly, and the usual
factories all up and down my arms.

They look this morning
as if they think their work is almost done;
some have already stepped back from the edge,
confident now that their welfare attention can be over.

I wish I were as sure
that in just a minute the power would go on,
lights light up, machinery hum, rivers flow

to their seas under our sky, and I stand
and walk right out of my grave, waving up
at my grandfather's smile
and tipping my hat to the sky.

The White Water Brule River Draught

If you think you can just
open your mouth
and swallow this river down,
and not have it
change your life,
you can forget it.
It's not going to just
meander through your throat,
your neck and chest,
belly and sex,
soak your legs
and dribble on out
of your feet.

No!
You chug this river
and it'll redo you.

It'll scour your mind,
whirl through your throat,
shout through your chest,
eddy in your belly,
flashflood your sex,
power on over
the edge of your hips,
cascade down
through your pillars
of leg, and finally
crash at your feet,
flinging up
mountains of mist
you will walk on
for days with maybe,
if you're lucky,
a rainbow's end
in each hand.

III. 2000's

The Green Sweater

St. Mary's, 6th Floor Psychiatric, 1966

I remember watching a cigarette burning skin
black between two deeply yellowed fingers
on my right hand as if it were someone else's hand.
I remember being puzzled by two tracks of smoke
stains beneath my nostrils on someone else's
face in the mirror. I remember walking my head
as if it were on someone else's shoulders
down a hall and back for what they told me
was two nights and the day between
with tears running out the first night.
I remember knitting my fingers
through the heavy steel mesh
surrounding the balcony, half-glad
and half-sorry I couldn't fall.

The Rochester streets were wet and dark with early November.
All day it was twilight outside. I pressed my forehead against it.

I remember begging to be knocked out
before I hurt somebody.
I remember throwing a doctor into a wall
and wrecking a room. I remember
a little dark-haired nurse, who wasn't afraid of me,
put her small hand gently on my right arm
and say, O.K. I'll go get it.
I remember waking up without my clothes
in the locked room, getting up ashamed,
but suddenly finding myself inside of God.
I remember knowing for sure I had lost
every good thing about me but believed him
when he said he still loved what was left.
I remember taking off the stinking green sweater
I'd worn a whole month when he told me
it wasn't the last chapter of my life.

For Sure

The world I live in is not a foreign country.
You know the same nights turning to morning.
The carrousel of birds circling your house.
The sounds of early-shift traffic, tires over concrete,
engine rev and gear strain measured through mufflers,
perhaps a near train and its "Hey! Move it!" whistle.
It's O.K. We are in this together. White houses
appear first. Distant water looks like gray shingles.
Don't worry. You will understand this poem enough.
You know what a knife at the throat feels like.
We needn't use it.

Once a woman put her hands on my head
while my father was dying. She touched
my eyes, and said they were like stones.
She gently rubbed my eyes and temples.
I prayed for God to take care of things.
My head went hot as warmed oil, burning
the woman's fingers. She had to leave the room.
The world I live in is not a foreign country.
Women and God come that close. Fathers leave,
allowed to die, their eyes becoming stones.
Eyes that are already stones become eyes again.
Knives are put away, back in their drawers.

Out my window you can see long grass
in need of mowing and in the garden at least
three colors of tulips are opening for sure.

Just Outside of Town

Fallujah mosque, November 13, 2004

The shotgun goes off in a string of three blasts.
I am the deer, the rifled slugs, the gun and the man
who pulled the trigger—this is plain enough.

The M-4 fires,
from six feet away, a single round
into the head of an already wounded Iraqi
lying in a room as dark as distance.
I am the foot that slumps to the floor,
his head, the high-speed bullet, the rifle, the man
who pulled the trigger, and the man who said,
"Well, he's dead now." It is hard to believe I am
all these things and a man only happens once.

"He could have been booby-trapped."

The cleanest war dirties the mind with understanding.

Hearing Loddigs Died

Drops of rain on the window. Surely tears.
I am all caught up in thinking of trout.
The rain gets done and birds are busy on the lawn.
My wife talks to me. It is not her fault
that she does not know where I am.
What kind of man must I be in her mind?
Finally it seems very important to look
the way I feel, but I can't. I say,
"You do not know where I am."
I turn the computer off,
find a clipboard and coffee, and head upstairs.
I become hungry for every concrete thing I see:
my bag of carving tools, a clothespin,
our envelope of taxes, a hand print on a window.
Going by, I pick up my short-wave radio.
I don't know why. Loddigs was over eighty,
a crumpled grocery bag of flesh
his spirit walked about through all last year.
I don't know why my wife doesn't know
where I am up here. We are closer than she thinks.
She in her third hour on the phone and I
listening hard to foreign language on the radio.

A Benediction for Seeing

Once upon a time
you will take off your shoes
and not put them on again.

You will look at yourself in the mirror
as if from the ceiling and say,
"Who is that person? That sad old thing?"

The shades you pull down on your day then
won't go up again. They will be the walls
of your room where you will be the only light
you need to see all the way to China.

Oh, later your hands will pluck up
invisible lint or threads from your sheets
and you'll pick plums and angels out of the air
and pat them aside, out of harm's way.

Then entire days of your entire life will come,
not to visit but to stay. Your hands will grip
the sides of your bed as you become the hero
of what no one else can do for you.

You alone will grasp it all, the edges of your life,
squeezing all that it meant and all that it just was
tighter and tighter into the two small spheres
of your eyes, looking out and shining,
until they become dull in the face
you are gone from.

Snow on Snow

remembering Alun Howells, nephew, 20, killed in Baghdad

Blue spruce boughs are weighted to the ground.
This is like plenty. This is like loss.

People we love become a place in us—
a place to go as soon as they are gone.

First there is the grieving, sometimes wailing.
Once I heard a cry cross streets of night,
fill the corners of every room, empty the air
from every good memory, and drop the glass
of a future, exploding across the floor.

Some try to stop their ears with money.
Others feel their souls cleaned into loving more.

I won't talk much more today.

I will go place a new birdfeeder on the trellis
where I can see it out the window
and fill it with thistle, millet, and safflower seeds
that call as many kinds of birds to alight
as I can count. I will say that each bird
is a loved one lost and found, come back.
I will say that this morning's evergreen boughs
are weighted not with loss but plenty—
all these beautiful places filling with light.

Standing in the Middle of My Life

Down this road above my Mississippi,
along Lake Pepin, I have often walked
but never seen what I have seen today.
Down the steep bank through sumac reds
and past the ash and willow yellows,
impossibly swimming in cold October water,
were all the people I can't forgive
and all who I fear can't forgive me.

And they all were happy, wet with forgiveness,
all glad to be wearing the same robe of water.
They were all one and all was forgiven.

But how could I trust their faces
calling me into the same water they swam in?
How could I let their water flow over me?
How can forgiving and being forgiven be the same?
How can both cover me as it covers them,
as is the nature of water?

How could I have stood and just watched?

The Undersides of Pelican Wings Are Black

Wild plum trees' thorny branches
have lost their softening leaves.

Frost that browns the grasses
stretches a skin over standing water.

Geese and swans and black-winged pelicans
have all sung their way to warmer homes.

Why is this morning's sunlight gray?

All around the edges of my life
the winds begin to question.

I have become the solitary
ghost in every room.

There is no bitter solace
that this is someone else's fault.

I am simply the branch,
the leaves, the grass, the standing water,
the shape in a departed nest.

The Beatitudes

Blessed are you who have seen all beyond you
    as *Achtung* in a country you don't know.

Blessed are you who have known what it's like
    to sit down inside your eyes and not come out.

Blessed are you who have known the bare mattress
    on the floor of a mind that made everyone
    think they could stand over you.

Blessed are you who have known the four walls of that mind
    slowly with the palms of your hands while the mental ward world
    changed your name to "you" by noon and by evening to "him."

Blessed are you who have felt that no matter where in the world,
    you may never have lived outside of this room.

Blessed are you who know your tears flow down the face of God.

No One As Alive
in memoriam

Like birds flying up
at a shotgun blast.
Like a fresh flower
withering back into a bud.
Like the thud of a deer
hitting a car.
Like the sound of footsteps
following you.
Like hearing voices
from underwater.
Like the ears' roar of holding
your breath too long.
Like the groan of the rafter
you hung yourself from.

All were the last split-second
of your fifteen-year-old life—
so tired of being yourself,
so tired of walking alone,
so tired of being the weed
in the yard that you pulled
yourself out and left it up
to your family to scream
open-mouthed with no sound
coming out that made sense—
the last "No!" said to you.

No one meant for you
to erase your life and leave
no one as alive that day
as your exclamation mark
upside down
and hanging in the air.

A Lighter Song

The pale blue November sky is washed with bronze
on the eastern horizon while the sun is still
behind the bluffs, and as it rises the white lace
curtains turn into transparent gold almost too bright
to look at, and the birds in my chest fly up
to meet the day with a gratitude that leaves
the heavy rest of me behind wondering if
the barren self will again conceive and bring to birth
a song as light as those birds weaving in and out
of bare branches networked against the sky like bars.

The Wind Gusting

The wind gusting to forty or fifty miles an hour
rocks tree trunks, the way boxers move
from the waist in the early, probing, less dire rounds.
Branches paw and test the air. Roots stretch but hold.
I see this slowly as I say it, passing it on to you.

And are you, too, like I am, hanging on?
The storm has lasted long, many rounds.
My head snaps back on its exhausted neck.
My waist, my legs, have lost all strategy.
I am a face slapped. I am dangling arms
with hands so stiff they can't even make change,
hold an egg, button a shirt, brush my hair,
or touch with the curve of my palms
someone's cherished face, and here I cry.

Let angels weep as well. They cannot know
desire, our body's grip on earth with legs
long numb that do not seem to stand a chance
to stand or move away from punishments of taking it
and taking it, while we sing failure's love song
sweeter than they can hear or understand.

Over There the Sun Shines

Over there the sun shines
through a small gap in the clouds.
It makes a gold circle of heaven
on the frozen, snow-covered lake.
Driving further down the road,
I see there are holes in the shelf of ice
over Isabella Creek that show her dark water
has been flowing lower and lower all winter long.
As I drive up to higher ground, clouds
have cleared, and the sun shines all over,
even over the black memories still circling
within my skull like water curling in an eddy.

Maybe this year, even in a few months,
the sun will come down deep enough
to clearly show that there is solid, level
limestone in me, flat bed of a decent
fishing stream that I can stand in.
Maybe this year, the sun-warmed water
will invite me into myself, and I will go,
and the stream will not float to me my old
dead faces, but instead, release hungry trout—
to move like living water, sides glimmering
with the light shining down into my blood.

There Comes a Time

Late February, early Spring, Northern Wisconsin

There comes a time when you have to go outside
and notice something: the lace edge of an undercut
patch of snow thawing or the uncovered still-green
fern leaves of yarrow or the furred lamb's ear,
the stubby fingers of sedum, the praying leaves of iris,
green flames of daisy leaf or tiny hands of rue.

There comes a time for the heart not to be a river
but just to be a sign of something melting
on a hillside facing south. Just a simple seeping in,
then puddling, meandering, just a going anywhere,
sliding on its own self is what heart wants.

Because too long a man's heart can be a stone
of winter, ice unable to think of root or flower
or even shiny pebbles wet with light. But this time
this heart, this man stands up and hears
the songs of birds becoming keys
unlocking something bright
to go outside and be.

At the Door

This slate-blue river is a green going,
a promise of paradise around the bend
that fills me enough to stay in the skin
and do my solemn dance of "I'll not die."

All this from a river on a morning's
first sunny day in a month wrapping every
contradictory bone of my body with
forgiveness for dropping so many leaves
in June and budding out so much in October
and living such a colorless life in between.

But now is the river, and now is the sun on skin.
Now is feeling again the true love of my senses.
This is no time to feel like my dog looks
when he thinks I'm mad at him. Instead my soul
says to me, "Do you want to go for a walk?"

And I am down on the floor with back arched
and front paws stretching out and the God
of real water and sunshine says to me,
"All right then! Let's do it!" Right out the door.

And Be Still

The sunrise gold
through birch and poplar leaves
on October 9th near Canada
is unbearable.
You can't keep looking at it—
so much hammered bronze,
brass, and red iron all around.

Even when you look down
at the path before you,
it's painted by Gustav Klimpt—
brilliant ovals of light.

Though you can turn your back,
you'd still know it's there.

Could we all be hardwired
to be stunned by autumn leaves?

It's true, although I have grieved,
and, at times, as alone as the moon,
I have not wanted to be,
I've never known an ugly sunrise.

But this morning, I am up and laugh
to have to turn so half-way away
from this too much glory, this
ache to thank a God.

The Bone White Oval Room

See a crow on a branch of gray poplar.
Imagine the bone white oval room of his brain.
What goes on in there all the day long?
What are his dreams? Plump carrion lying dead
safely away from dangerous highways?
How about how the children are doing?
Do they have children? I've never seen
a small crow. They're all the same size
with that identical cut black paper look.
How long is their workday? Do they rest?
Do they admit they should work harder
or pretend they're doing more than their share?
How about grudges? Can they forgive?
Do they have a loving god or just more tearing flesh?
Is their god a big white crow or a blacker than black one?
Do they know they should pray more?
Does time pass quickly and sometimes slower, too?
Do they think of death? Do they hoard food?
Is everything that goes through that room
just appetite's service to survival?
Are they concerned about the needs of others?
Do they suppose, "I should have gotten more"?
Do they regret someone's presence in their life?
Do they believe sometimes, "I made the wrong choices"?
Do they have nightmares or get depressed?
Do they seek Truth? Beauty? Morality? Pleasure?
Mercy? Justice? In themselves or somewhere else?
Does this one keep on thinking of how his wife looked
that time in the elm tree with the sun setting behind her?
If not all this in their brains every day,
what then lives in that bone white oval room?

Seeing True Green

Funny how sharp green the grass
and simple blue the sky
and ancient red the pump handle still looks
and aching cold the water feels as it
splashes the bare feet of a young boy
standing with his first wasp bite,
watching his uncle smooth mud on his flaming arm
to make it better and "suck the poison out"
while his older brother assures him that the wasp
must have been a black one, the worst kind, the kind
that can kill you if it bites too close to a vein,
which, of course, makes the boy's whole body a vein,
an easy target, until he remembers his uncle loves him
very much and doesn't look worried at all
and even is smiling a little though he doesn't say a thing

because he loves the boy's brother, too,
and remembers he, himself, didn't even have a brother,
but it was his cousins, one already dead now—
his favorite—who told him about the deadly wasps,
and, in his turn, helped him see true green
and blue and red and feel real cold.

Grandma Graber's Braid

During the day, Grandma wore her hair braided up
and, though long widowed, she always wore black.
But one night when I was ten and she was visiting,
I saw her by accident. She was turned half-away
from her bedroom door with a table lamp behind her.
Almost down to her waist—she was brushing hair
as achingly beautiful as only a boy could see,
not being a man. Then I saw the light change,
glow through her thin, white flannel nightgown
through the door that framed her shape
that amazed me—like a woman's it was—
with breasts, a waist, and real hips as far
as I could tell, and she was humming softly.
I couldn't let her see me, and she didn't.

I told my mother later only about the hair.
She said that Grandma brushed it out every night
and oddly for a woman of sixty-three left it loose.
I didn't tell Mom it wasn't odd at all and how it still
sounded like Grandma was humming just for me.

Crystal Clear

I cannot recall the time of year.
I remember it as if we were within a sphere,
the kind that snows when turned.
It wasn't winter, my sleeves were rolled,
and I was fifteen and playing the love song
from *Exodus* with one hand that really didn't know
how to play our new, blond upright piano.
My mother was in the kitchen behind the divider wall,
and we were talking forgettable threads of thought
that amiably were started and then dropped to pick up
another in casual fingers. It was after school and no one
else was home, and I played again and again that little song
I had figured out—one note of melody at a time.
It was a conversation I did not know I was having

with my mother right there under all the talk of school
and after awhile she got silent and me babbling on,
and then she came into the living room where I was,
and she was drying her hands on a dishtowel—
the late afternoon light was behind her, and her hair
looked really nice, and she said, "You know, John,
I chose your father, but I didn't choose you . . .
you children will go, and I will be with your father again."
And that was that. She said it eerie cold.
My hands froze above the keys.
All of a sudden a door closed and she
was inside a crystal globe, forever beautiful,
and I was standing on the outside, turned upside down
and righted, all alone with what seemed to fall like snow.

Up the Ladder

So I'm sixty years old and standing on a ladder
sanding the spackled mesh over the ceiling cracks,
hands up, neck bent back, shoulder muscles knotted
up into my ears, and my wife comes halfway
through the doorway as if it's an afterthought:
"I love you *so* much," she says, ". . . *so* much."
And then she's gone. What is there left to do?

Ascend into heaven? She said it like in a blue ribbon
dream at twenty, in bed, her voice sung down a third.
What is there left to do? She said it.

From all across the room she brought her opal eyes
home to me. There on the ladder, I had her,
and she had me walking away. Who knows?
At twenty or sixty sex can come or go,
but for this aging man in his aging room,
up the ladder, love remains, sum after sum
with no need for calculation.

Only on This Planet
January 8, Northern Wisconsin

When late afternoon sunlight
comes in low over the land
on a blue day after an ice storm,
only on this planet can you see
stubble fields littered with sapphire.
Only here can you look through one ridge
of ice-bent birch-barked trees
to another higher ridge behind it,
with the sun behind them both,
and see the quivering silver chain mail links
of the highest angel, Michael,
sequin with his every move, like wind
flattering autumn aspen. And only on this earth
are there oaks and hickories strong enough
to laugh triumphant under crystal ice
while arching it up on limbs flaunting high
the weight of their lace palaces of beauty.
Here alone is the place where even the fringes
on the hedgerows stun, and the dark red
of the stop signs warm so much, the sun
drips down from them in cut glass tears.
But that's not sad. Not here. Not now.
Not for any of us left on this only planet blessed
with ice storms with mostly happy endings.

Feeding Birds in Winter

Fearless black-capped chickadees,
crabby blue jays, flocks of tentative
frumpy sparrows, crowds of cardinals
with their ladies looking like cedar wax wings,
juncos in dark, fitted sport coats and light khakis,
a single no-way! blue bird, a fat-chance! purple finch,
and one downy-billed woodpecker standing out
like a red, white, and black flag—
all in one berserkly overgrown forsythia bush,
more or less taking turns around a hanging
birdfeeder full of oil black sunflower seeds
to save life in January. Beautiful.

Then a Sharp-shinned Hawk took to roosting
in the volunteer pine right off the porch.
Beautiful. Long, white chest speckled
rust-brown like the robin-cousin thrush,
slender with a barred chisel of a tail
and a compact, elegant, gray head, smooth
around small, red eyes and short, strong beak that—
this morning, right out the kitchen window
ten feet away—pinned down
my struggling woodpecker
to the white, compressed snow path,
pecked short feathers from its skull
as it tried to turn away, as body feathers stood out
askew like sweat-spiked hair and its long, thin bill
scissored open and closed in a kind of drowning,
those careless feathers finally going still
as the hawk's beak broke through the skull
for the first part eaten, brain fat
for the hawk's own weather.

By then, gun in hand, what could I do
but yell him safely away from me—
two birds beautifully rising.

Green Fire

Sitting on the breathing porch,
cheerful air places its palms
on my western cheek.

An apple on the table
is dreaming of an orchard,
and so am I.

My eyes look down,
and I begin to see
my hands
and bless the scars
that didn't kill me.

I haul memories around
in auras of their light.

Death's grip
on me weakens.

A frown falls to the floor.

Fear staggers off
and drops like
a drunk in a snowdrift.

Tonight is a patch
of goodness, grace,
thought lost,
turning towards me.

I tell you,
I am drinking
warm twilight
through my pores.

Tonight, As Always, It Is Hard to Die
Late November

Low on the horizon the crescent moon

rolls over on its back and laughs,
like a happy child rocking
with its feet in the air,

nesting in a soft ring of thick light
that glows through a loose cradle
of winter-woven black walnut branches.

Light snows slowly on the pale dry grass.

Lord, let my last breath be big enough
to hold all this and you.

The Large Small Dog Speaks

My father was horse.
I was born in a field.
My mother was cow.
Somehow it happened,
and I am a dog.
My mother loved my father,
who never belonged here
but fell from somewhere out of the sky
to be with my mother who loved him.
He could jump so high, and when he'd run
his feet never touched the ground—
if you looked, you could see it.
My father loved my mother,
who grew up out of the ground
to be with my father who loved her.
She couldn't jump but ran sometimes
though her feet never left the ground—
she was ground and a lap and a stable
out of the wind for my father.
I was born in a field.
Somehow it happened,
and I am a dog.

For my bark, my voice, and its encouragement, I thank my family of origin: Paul & Harriet Nelson Graber, Anya, Paul & Steph, and Jaena & Gwyn.

I thank my wife, Elise, and our children, Josh, Sam, Lucy & Andy and granddaughter Kristina, for being many-colored graces to me—as well as great crap-detectors.

I thank William Stafford, fellow Western Kansan, for his essay, "A Way of Writing," that taught me *how to write*.

I thank the wealth of teachers I've been lucky enough to have in person: David Wee, who tuned me up for two great years with Marvin Bell, Donald Justice, Richard Hugo, and Norman Dubie; later, Michael Dennis Brown; and, now, Mary Logue—all of whom taught me *how to rewrite* my private language more clearly into readers' memories, hearts, and minds.

Thanks to Jim Bodeen, my editor at Blue Begonia Press, who heard, understood, and welcomed what I was doing more than I could have asked for or imagined.

Notes

p. 31 While in St. Peter's Rome — This poem comes from the same year as the "Volkschule, 1955" poem of vengeance. The same boy is the speaker, yet the tone is that of an epiphany of the holy. Michelangelo's Pieta the famous sculpture in St. Peter's Cathedral, shows Mary looking as young as her son, the crucified Jesus. For five hundred years, believers on pilgrimage to Rome could reach just high enough to reverently touch Jesus' feet for a blessing, wearing them down like the stone stairs in old buildings. I saw this when I was nine, and it inspired a vision I can't forget.

p. 32 "Say It Again, Daddy!" — According to *National Geographic*, the recorded song of the humpback whale when sped up 17 times sounds just like birdsong. Hearing delightful proof from a little freebie phonograph record mailed inside an issue of NG, coupled with a stern demand from my six-year-old son, "Won't you ever write a poem a kid can read!" brought this poem into being.

About the Artists:

Lucy Stoyke

Lucy Stoyke lives in Wyoming, Minnesota, with her husband, Andy, and their daughter, Kristina. Currently her creative process involves raising children, but she also works at writing, editing, and art when she can. She credits her time in the 1990s at the Grünewald Guild in Plain, Washington, for renewing her faith to make art and for showing her more clearly the relationship between art and faith. "Grace upon Grace", a stained glass piece, was created there in 1996 with Joe Hester's guidance and teaching (and access to his amazing stash of glass). It is still the only work in stained glass that Lucy has made, and she finds the choice of it for the cover another example of grace upon grace.

Midge Bolt

Photographer Midge Bolt has had a camera in her hands since she was 11, when her uncle gave her his Polaroid Swinger camera. Her fascination with old photos was the inspiration for her TIME & AGAIN® artwork, in which she layers an old photo printed on sheer fabric in front of her own present day photo of the same scene. The viewer looks through the ephemeral image from long ago into the scene as it appears today. Midge lives in Wisconsin with her architect husband and two dogs in the house they designed and built on the bluffs above Lake Pepin. As a student in one of John's recent poetry writing workshops she was delighted to discover that she can also create images with words.

About the Author

I grew up in Western Kansas and graduated from Hays High in 1964. I received degrees from St. Olaf College in 1968 and the University of Iowa Writers Workshop in 1972. The physical labor that helped finance my education gave the white collar of my writing and teaching career an indelible blue tinge. During the 1970's at Holden Village in the North Cascades, I taught grades 1–12 in a one-room school and developed a college-level program called Life-Style Enrichment. After six years in Washington, my wife, Elise, and I returned to the Midwest with our **three young children to an old house** on the banks of the Mississippi, in the village of Stockholm, Wisconsin, where we've lived for three decades along with several beloved dogs.

After many good years, I retired from teaching English due to increased difficulty with bipolar-I mood disorder, which can complicate, interrupt, and sometimes shut down writing, editing, and **life in general.** Nevertheless, over 50 poems have been published, most in national magazines—The American Poetry Review, Iowa Review, and The American Review among them. Recently three chapbooks have been published, one an online collection.

In the last few years, during my healthy seasons, I have again enjoyed giving rousing readings, editing for beginning and published poets, and teaching my "Writing and Repair of Poetry" workshop. I also give presentations on "What Makes Poetry Work: Big Ideas of Poetry and Tricks of the Trade." I am developing a project using poetry and poetry writing for the mental health community.

John Graber

John Graber can be contacted at Box 639/ Stockholm, WI 54769.

ACKNOWLEDGMENTS

All publications are magazines; poems that also appear in the chapbooks listed below are marked with appropriate asterisks.

The American Poetry Review 1700 Miles to Elise
The American Review ★Northwest of Oslo
The Birdsong Review ★St. Mary's Psychiatric and ★While in St. Peter's, Rome
The Daily Iowan ★Reporting the Traumatization of Flesh
Fabbro (University of Kentucky) Making Change
Free Verse ★Kansas Steel and Stone Blues from the City, Tributes, ★★The Dance of the Robins, and ★"Not My Father"
The Great River Review ★A Letter, ★Pegasus, ★★Like Growing Potatoes, ★★Drinking America, and The Problem
The Iowa Review Like Land Used Up
The Journal of the American Medical Association (*JAMA*) The Dictionary of Anhedonia, Leaning Forward, and ★★Over There the Sun Shines
The Kansas Quarterly ★The Gift
The Madison Review ★The Blizzard
Poetry Northwest ★Volkschule, 1955 and ★Pledge
Rosebud ★Stable Fire in Time of War
Transactions—Wisconsin Poetry (An Anthology), reprinted 1700 Miles To Elise and Like Land Used Up
The Wisconsin Academy Review Hearing Loddigs Died
Wisconsin People & Ideas ★★Reach and ★★The White Water Brule River Draught
The Wisconsin Review ★Walking Home

★*Walking Home*, Pudding House Publications Chapbook, July 2007, published fourteen of the above poems, appearing entirely in Section I.
★★Only On This Planet, Parallel Press Chapbook Series, University of Wisconsin—Madison, September 2007, published six of the above poems and nineteen others in this book, appearing mostly in Section II.
Thanksgiving Dawn (an on-line Poetry Pole chapbook sharing this book's title), Blue Begonia Press, published thirteen poems in this book, appearing mostly in Section III.